To:

May you have a heart full of hugs
every day!

From:

Requests for information should be addressed to:
  Inspirio, The gift group of Zondervan
  Grand Rapids, Michigan 49530
  http://www.inspiriogifts.com

Associate Editor and Compiler: Molly C. Detweiler
Project Manager: Patricia Matthews
Design: Mark Veldheer

Printed in China
03 04/❖ HK/ 4 3 2

Heartful of Hugs

inspirio™

Faith is knowing
there is an ocean
because you have
seen a brook.

Because of the LORD's great
love we are not consumed,
for his compassions
never fail.
They are new every morning;
great is your faithfulness.

Lamentations 3:22–23

A friend is one who helps
you do your best.

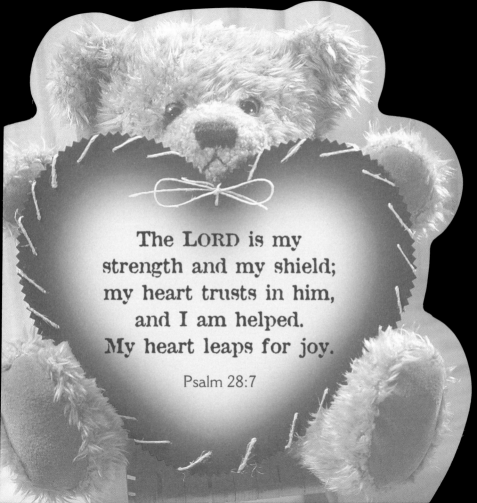

The LORD is my
strength and my shield;
my heart trusts in him,
and I am helped.
My heart leaps for joy.

Psalm 28:7

Life is like a mirror—we get the best results when we smile at it.

The LORD blesses his
people with peace.

Psalm 29:11

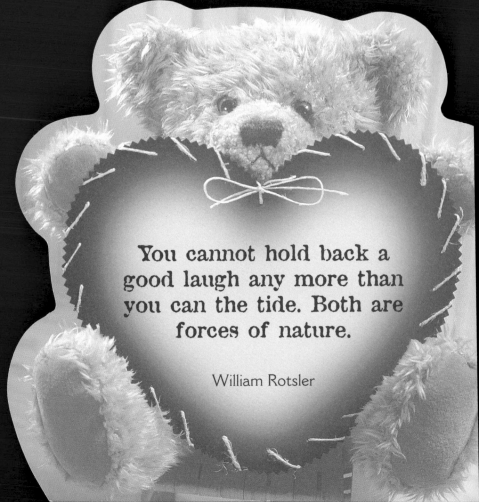

You cannot hold back a good laugh any more than you can the tide. Both are forces of nature.

William Rotsler

Your love has given
me great joy and
encouragement.

Philemon 7

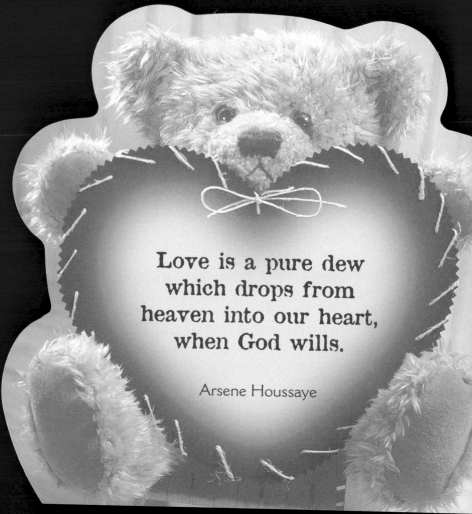

Love is a pure dew
which drops from
heaven into our heart,
when God wills.

Arsene Houssaye

May God give you of heaven's dew and of earth's richness.

Genesis 27:28

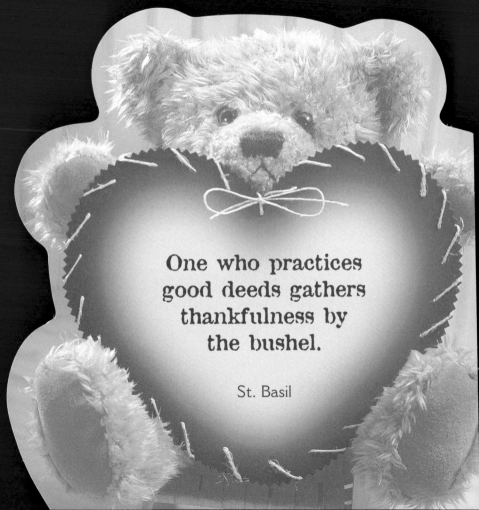

One who practices good deeds gathers thankfulness by the bushel.

St. Basil

We are God's workmanship, created in Christ Jesus to do good works, which God prepared in advance for us to do.

Ephesians 2:10

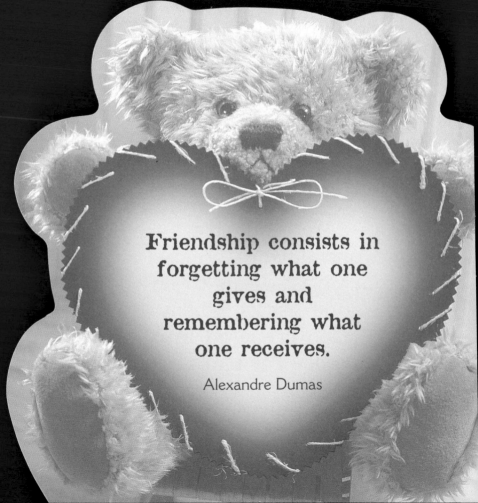

Friendship consists in
forgetting what one
gives and
remembering what
one receives.

Alexandre Dumas

Jesus said, "Everyone who asks receives; he who seeks finds; and to him who knocks, the door will be opened."

Matthew 7:8

Whoever loves true life,
loves true love.

Elizabeth Barrett Browning

Love never fails.

1 Corinthians 13:8

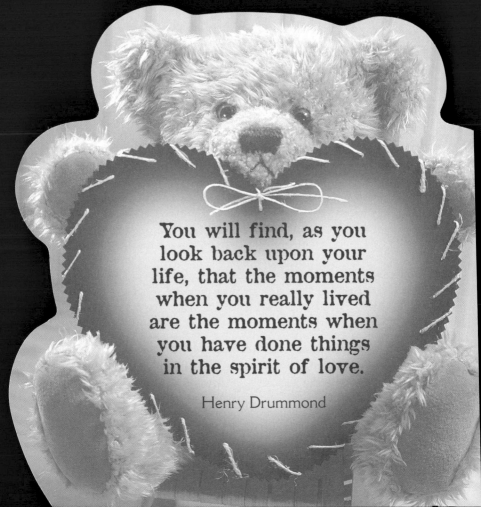

You will find, as you look back upon your life, that the moments when you really lived are the moments when you have done things in the spirit of love.

Henry Drummond

Do everything
in love.

1 Corinthians 16:14

You learn to love
by loving.

Frances de Sales

May the Lord make your love increase and overflow for each other and for everyone else.

1 Thessalonians 3:12

The soul that walks
in love neither tires
others nor grows
tired.

John of the Cross

Let us not become weary in doing good, for at the proper time we will reap a harvest if we do not give up.

Galatians 6:9

Love teaches even flowers
to dance.

French Proverb

"The maidens will dance
and be glad,
young men and old as well.
I will turn their mourning
into gladness;
I will give them comfort and
joy instead of sorrow," says
the Lord.

Jeremiah 31:13

The love of God is
like the Amazon
River flowing down
to water just
one daisy.

Author Unknown

"I will pour water on the thirsty land, and streams on the dry ground; I will pour out my Spirit on your offspring, and my blessing on your descendants. They will spring up like grass in a meadow, like poplar trees by flowing streams," says the LORD.

Isaiah 44:3–4

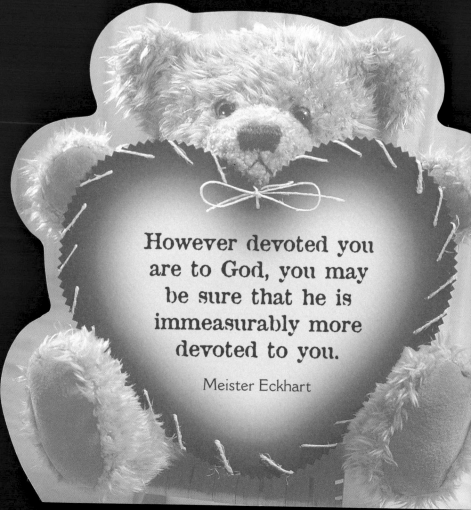

However devoted you
are to God, you may
be sure that he is
immeasurably more
devoted to you.

Meister Eckhart

This is how God
showed his love among
us: He sent his one and
only Son into the
world that we might
live through him.

1 John 4:9

To love another
person is to help
them love God.

Søren Kierkegaard

No one has ever seen
God; but if we love
one another, God
lives in us and his
love is made
complete in us.

1 John 4:12

He who counts the
stars and calls them
by their names is in
no danger of
forgetting His
own children.

C. H. Spurgeon

God determines the number
of the stars and calls
them each by name.
Great is our Lord and
mighty in power;
his understanding
has no limit.

Psalm 147:4–5

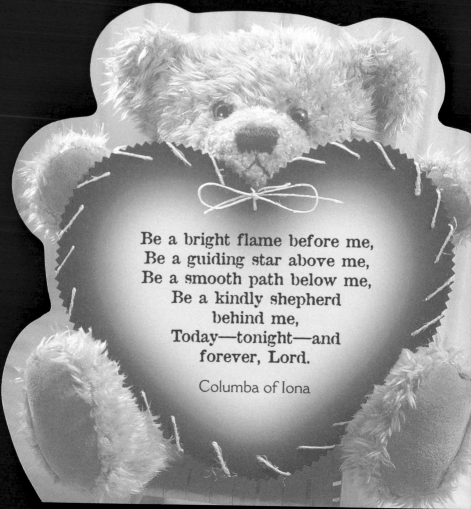

Be a bright flame before me,
Be a guiding star above me,
Be a smooth path below me,
Be a kindly shepherd
behind me,
Today—tonight—and
forever, Lord.

Columba of Iona

Send forth your light
and your truth,
let them guide me,
O LORD.

Psalm 43:3

The right kind of
heart is a kind heart
like God's.

Author Unknown

Dear friends, now we are children of God, and what we will be has not yet been made known. But we know that when Jesus appears, we shall be like him, for we shall see him as he is.

1 John 3:2

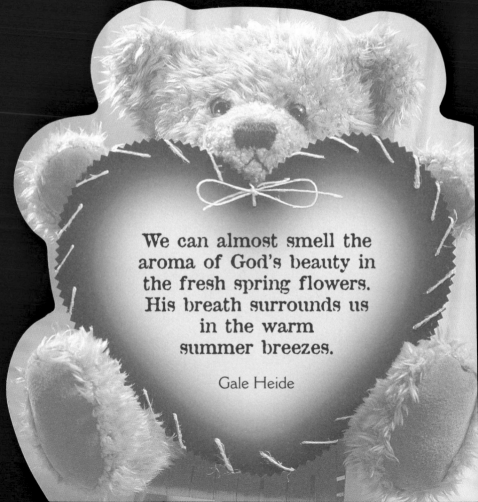

We can almost smell the
aroma of God's beauty in
the fresh spring flowers.
His breath surrounds us
in the warm
summer breezes.

Gale Heide

The Mighty One, God,
the LORD,
speaks and summons
the earth from the
rising of the sun to the place
where it sets.
From Zion, perfect in beauty,
God shines forth.

Psalm 50:1–2

We look forward to a time when the power of love will replace the love of power. Then will our world know the blessings of peace.

William Gladstone

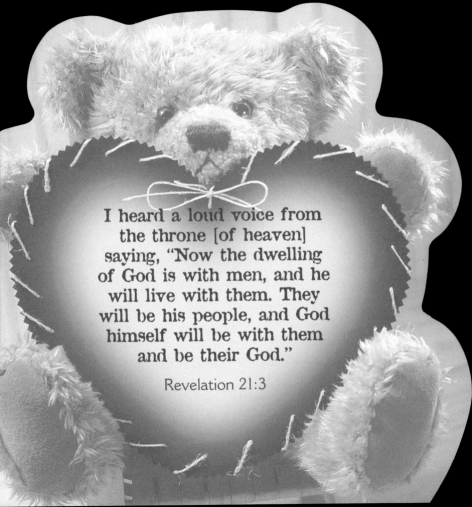

I heard a loud voice from the throne [of heaven] saying, "Now the dwelling of God is with men, and he will live with them. They will be his people, and God himself will be with them and be their God."

Revelation 21:3

The time to get your spiritual instrument in tune is early in the morning before the concert of the day begins.

Author Unknown

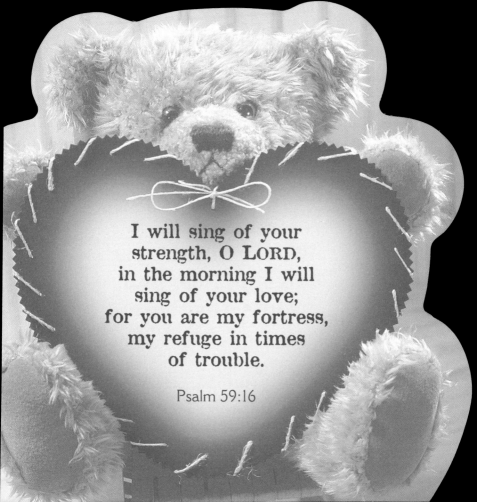

I will sing of your
strength, O LORD,
in the morning I will
sing of your love;
for you are my fortress,
my refuge in times
of trouble.

Psalm 59:16

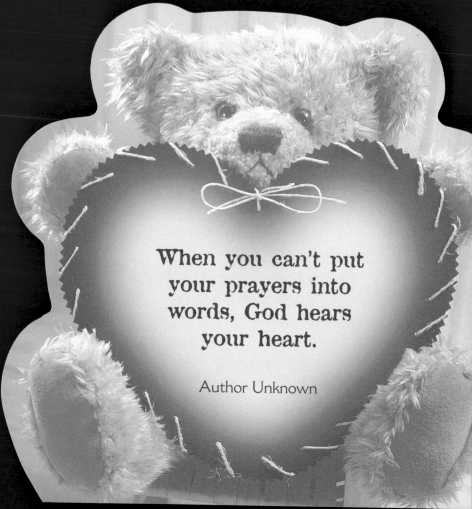

When you can't put
your prayers into
words, God hears
your heart.

Author Unknown

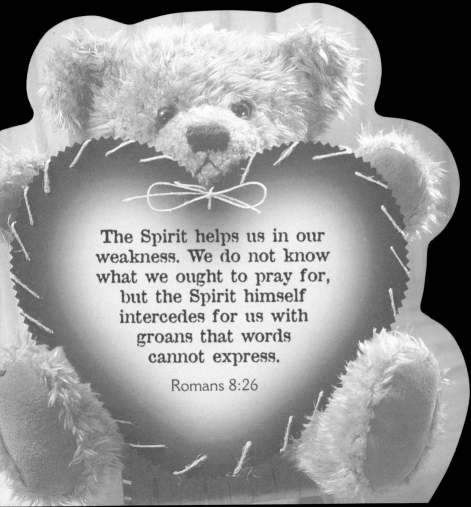

The Spirit helps us in our weakness. We do not know what we ought to pray for, but the Spirit himself intercedes for us with groans that words cannot express.

Romans 8:26

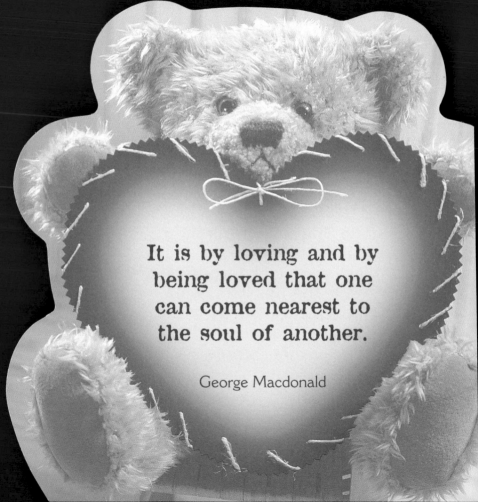

It is by loving and by being loved that one can come nearest to the soul of another.

George Macdonald

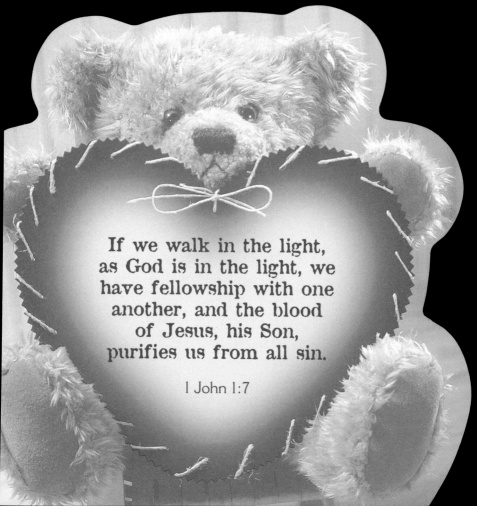

If we walk in the light,
as God is in the light, we
have fellowship with one
another, and the blood
of Jesus, his Son,
purifies us from all sin.

1 John 1:7

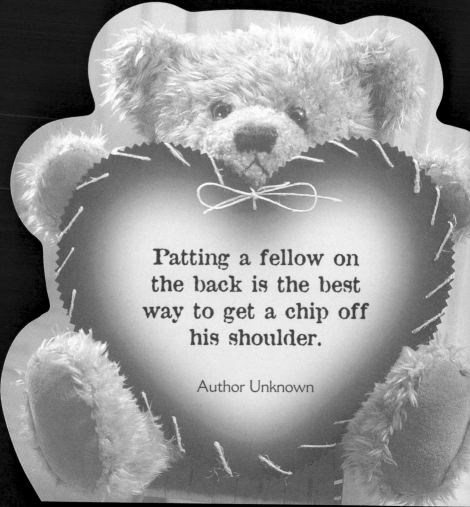

Patting a fellow on the back is the best way to get a chip off his shoulder.

Author Unknown

A gentle answer
turns away wrath.

Proverbs 15:1

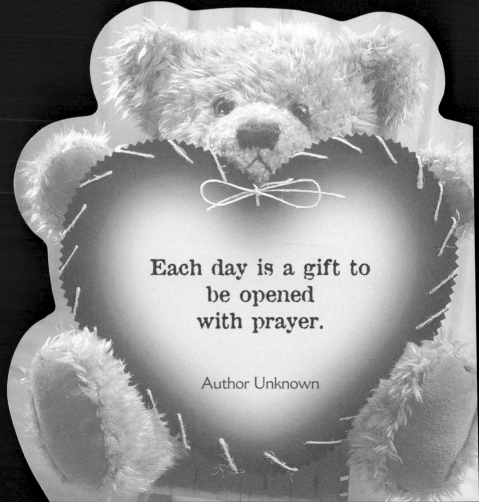

Each day is a gift to
be opened
with prayer.

Author Unknown

Where morning
dawns and
evening fades
you call forth songs
of joy, O Lord.

Psalm 65:8

God's gifts put
man's best dreams
to shame.

Elizabeth Barrett Browning

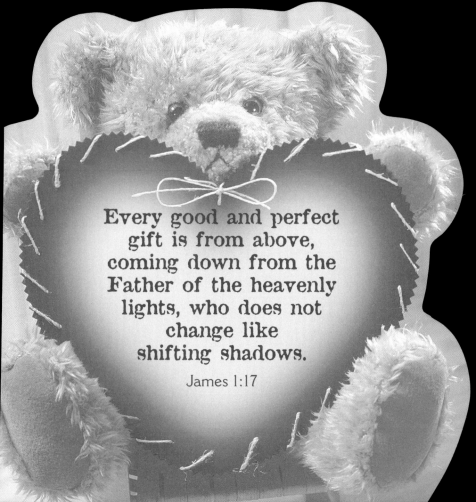

Every good and perfect gift is from above, coming down from the Father of the heavenly lights, who does not change like shifting shadows.

James 1:17

Jesus did not come
to make God's love
possible, but to make
God's love visible.

Author Unknown

Jesus is the image of
the invisible God, the
firstborn over all
creation. For by him
all things
were created.
Colossians 1:15–16

The really great
person is the person
who makes every
man feel great.

G. K. Chesterton

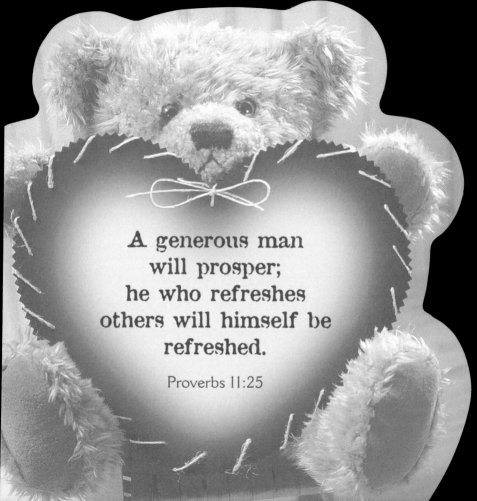

A generous man
will prosper;
he who refreshes
others will himself be
refreshed.

Proverbs 11:25

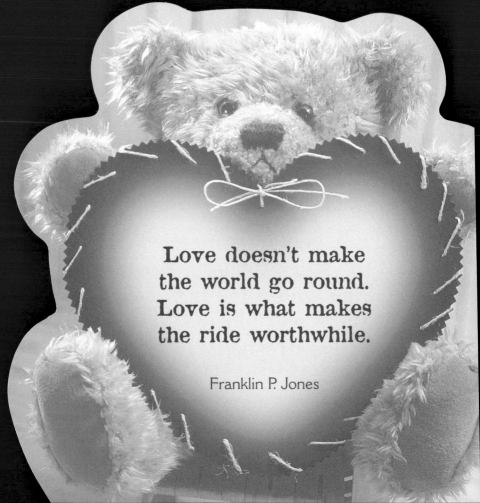

Love doesn't make
the world go round.
Love is what makes
the ride worthwhile.

Franklin P. Jones

These three remain:
faith, hope and love.
But the greatest of
these is love.

1 Corinthians 13:13

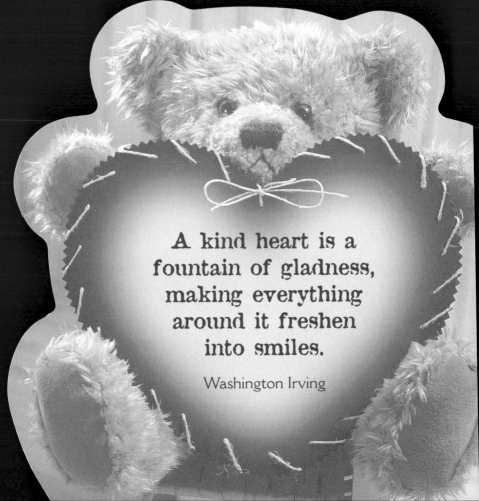

A kind heart is a fountain of gladness, making everything around it freshen into smiles.

Washington Irving

The mouth of the
righteous is a
fountain of life.

Proverbs 10:11

I will not wish thee riches,
Nor the glow of greatness,
But that wherever thou go
Some weary heart
Shall gladden at thy smile.

Inscription on the wall of a church
in Upwaltham, England

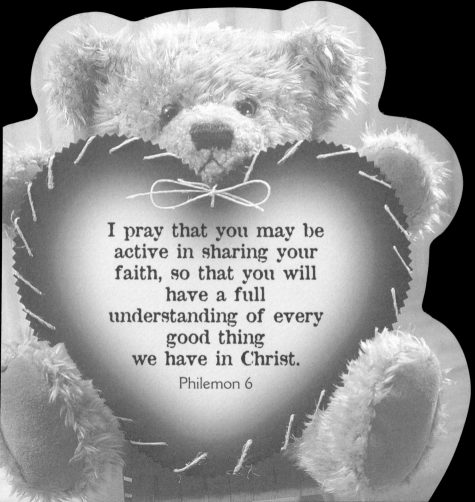

I pray that you may be active in sharing your faith, so that you will have a full understanding of every good thing we have in Christ.

Philemon 6

This is the miracle
that happens every
time to those who
really love; the more
they give, the more
they possess.

Rainer Maria Rilke

Give, and it will be given to you. A good measure, pressed down, shaken together and running over, will be poured into your lap. For with the measure you use, it will be measured to you.

Luke 6:38

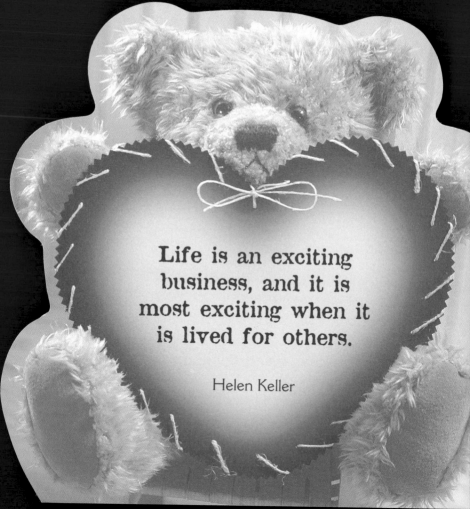

Life is an exciting business, and it is most exciting when it is lived for others.

Helen Keller

Greater love has no one than this, that he lay down his life for his friends.

John 15:13

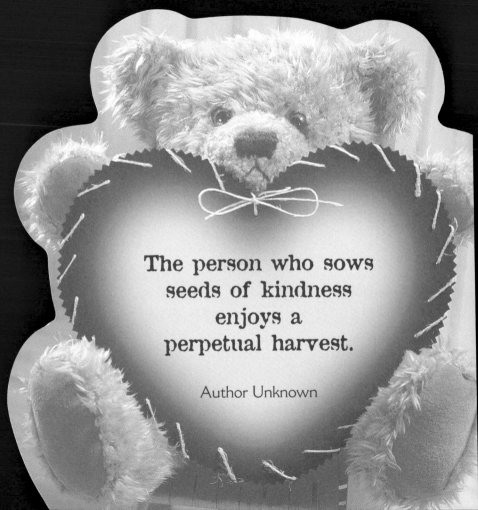

The person who sows
seeds of kindness
enjoys a
perpetual harvest.

Author Unknown

Peacemakers who
sow in peace
raise a harvest
of righteousness.

James 3:18

All love is sweet
Given or returned.
Common as light
is love,
And its familiar voice
wearies not ever.

Percy Bysshe Shelley

Love always protects,
always trusts,
always hopes,
always perseveres.

1 Corinthians 13:7

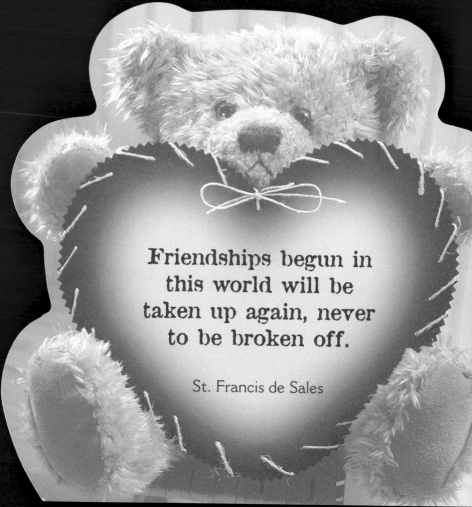

Friendships begun in this world will be taken up again, never to be broken off.

St. Francis de Sales

We believe that Jesus
died and rose again
and so we believe that
God will bring with
Jesus those who have
fallen asleep in him.

1 Thessalonians 4:14

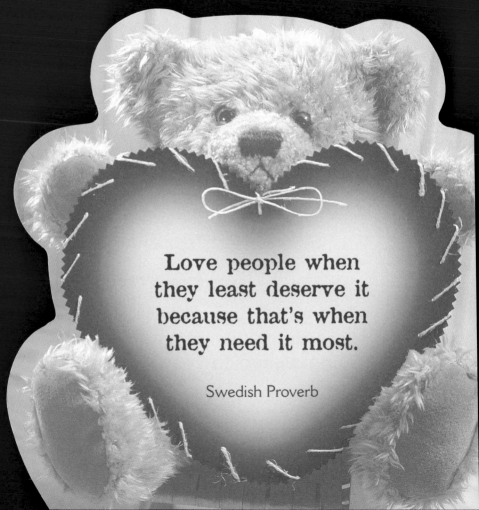

Love people when they least deserve it because that's when they need it most.

Swedish Proverb

Love your enemies, do good to them, and lend to them without expecting to get anything back. Then your reward will be great, and you will be sons of the Most High.

Luke 6:35

Angels can fly
because they take
themselves lightly.

G. K. Chesterton

Those who hope in
the LORD
will renew their strength.
They will soar on
wings like eagles;
they will run and
not grow weary,
they will walk and
not be faint.

Isaiah 40:31

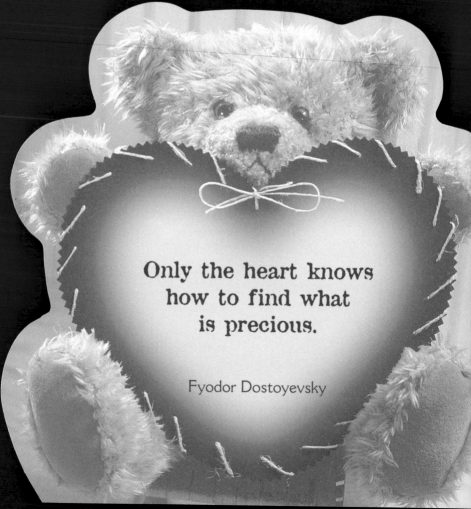

Only the heart knows
how to find what
is precious.

Fyodor Dostoyevsky

Above all else, guard
your heart, for it is
the wellspring of life.

Proverbs 4:23

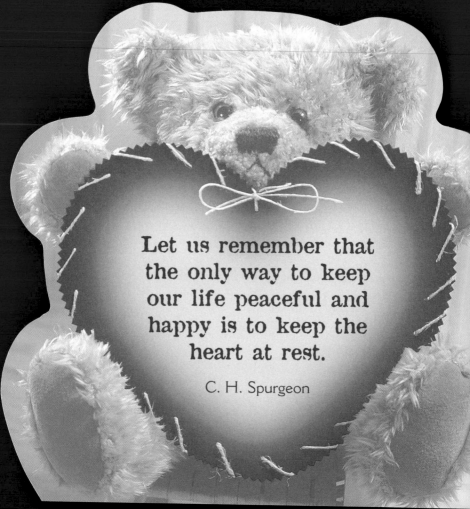

Let us remember that the only way to keep our life peaceful and happy is to keep the heart at rest.

C. H. Spurgeon

A heart at peace
gives life to the body.

Proverbs 14:30

There is not one
blade of grass, there
is no color in this
world that is not
intended to make
us rejoice.

John Calvin

Let the heavens rejoice,
let the earth be glad;
let the sea resound,
and all that is in it;
let the fields be jubilant,
and everything in them.
Then all the trees of the
forest will sing for joy;
they will sing before the LORD.

Psalm 96:11–13

Love shall be our token;
Love be yours
and love be mine;
Love to God
and all men,
Love for plea and gift
and sign.

Christina Rossetti

We know and rely on the love God has for us. God is love. Whoever lives in love lives in God, and God in him.

1 John 4:16

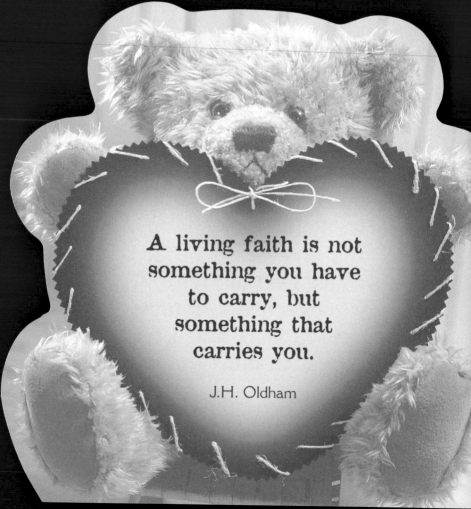

A living faith is not
something you have
to carry, but
something that
carries you.

J.H. Oldham

Everyone born of God overcomes the world. This is the victory that has overcome the world, even our faith.

1 John 5:4

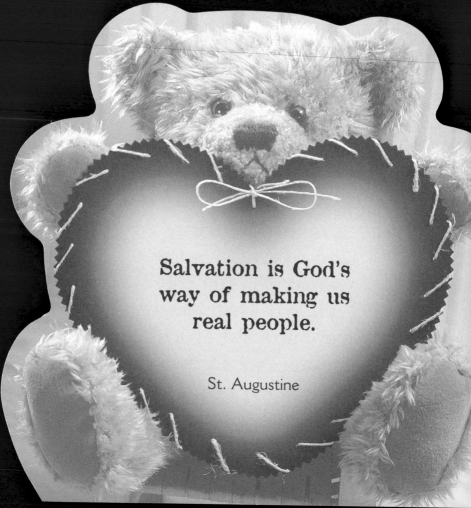

Salvation is God's
way of making us
real people.

St. Augustine

God made Christ who had no sin to be sin for us, so that in him we might become the righteousness of God.

2 Corinthians 5:21

As long as one can admire and love, then one is young for ever.

Pablo Casals

A cheerful heart is
good medicine.

Proverbs 17:22

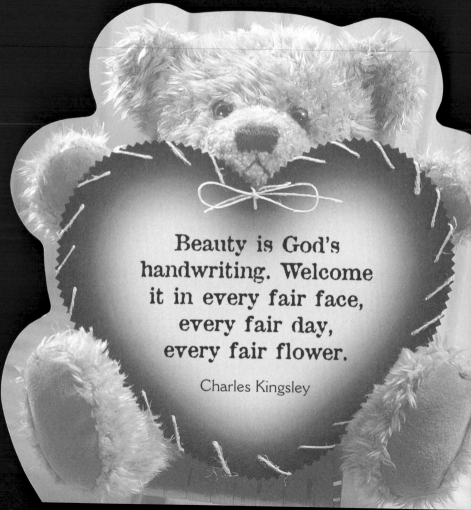

Beauty is God's
handwriting. Welcome
it in every fair face,
every fair day,
every fair flower.

Charles Kingsley

God has made
everything beautiful
in its time.

Ecclesiastes 3:11

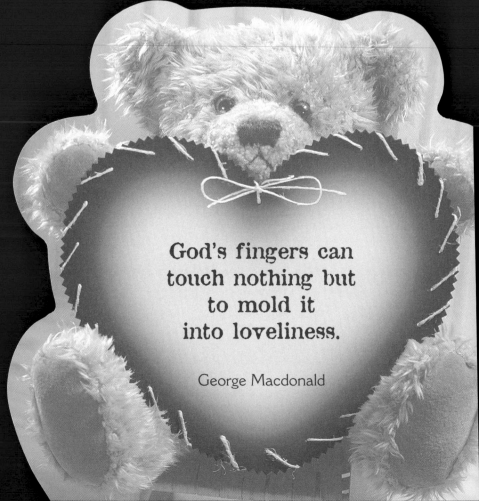

God's fingers can
touch nothing but
to mold it
into loveliness.

George Macdonald

God created man in his own image, in the image of God he created him; male and female he created them. ... God saw all that he had made, and it was very good.

Genesis 1:27, 31

Spread love
everywhere you go.
Be the living
expression of God's
kindness.

Mother Teresa

Thanks be to God, who always leads us in triumphal procession in Christ and through us spreads everywhere the fragrance of the knowledge of him.

2 Corinthians 2:14

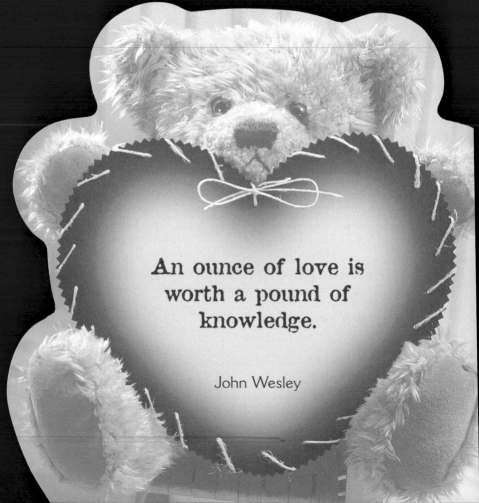

An ounce of love is worth a pound of knowledge.

John Wesley

Knowledge puffs up,
but love builds up.

1 Corinthians 8:1

He that lives in hope
dances without music.

George Herbert

I will always
have hope;
I will praise you
more and more,
O LORD.

Psalm 71:14

The thankful heart
will find, in
every hour, some
heavenly blessings.

Henry Ward Beecher

Give thanks to the LORD
for his unfailing love
and his wonderful
deeds for men,
for he satisfies the thirsty
and fills the hungry
with good things.

Psalm 107:8–9

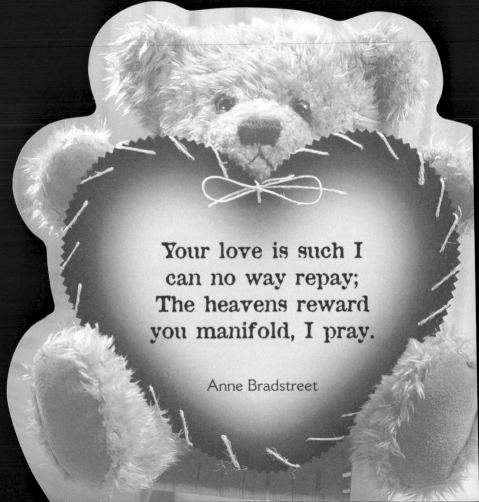

Your love is such I can no way repay; The heavens reward you manifold, I pray.

Anne Bradstreet

How can I repay
the LORD
for all his goodness
to me?
I will lift up the
cup of salvation
and call on the name of
the LORD.

Psalm 116:12–13

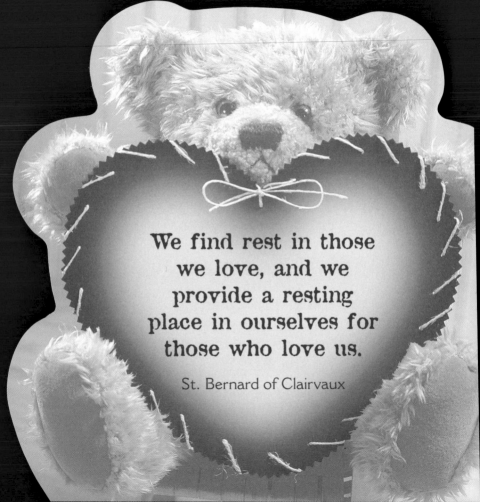

We find rest in those
we love, and we
provide a resting
place in ourselves for
those who love us.

St. Bernard of Clairvaux

Jesus said, "Come to me, all you who are weary and burdened, and I will give you rest."

Matthew 11:28

Have a heart that never hardens, and a temper that never tires, and a touch that never hurts.

Charles Dickens

Be completely
humble and gentle; be
patient, bearing with
one another in love.

Ephesians 4:2

Every blade of grass,
each leaf, each
separate petal, is an
inscription speaking
of hope.

Richard Jefferies

You answer us with awesome deeds
of righteousness, O God our Savior,
the hope of all the ends
of the earth....
You crown the year with your bounty,
and your carts overflow
with abundance.

Psalm 65:5, 11

Nothing is sweeter than Love, nothing stronger, nothing higher, nothing wider, nothing more pleasant, nothing fuller nor better in heaven and earth.

Thomas à Kempis

Love one another
deeply, from
the heart.

1 Peter 1:22

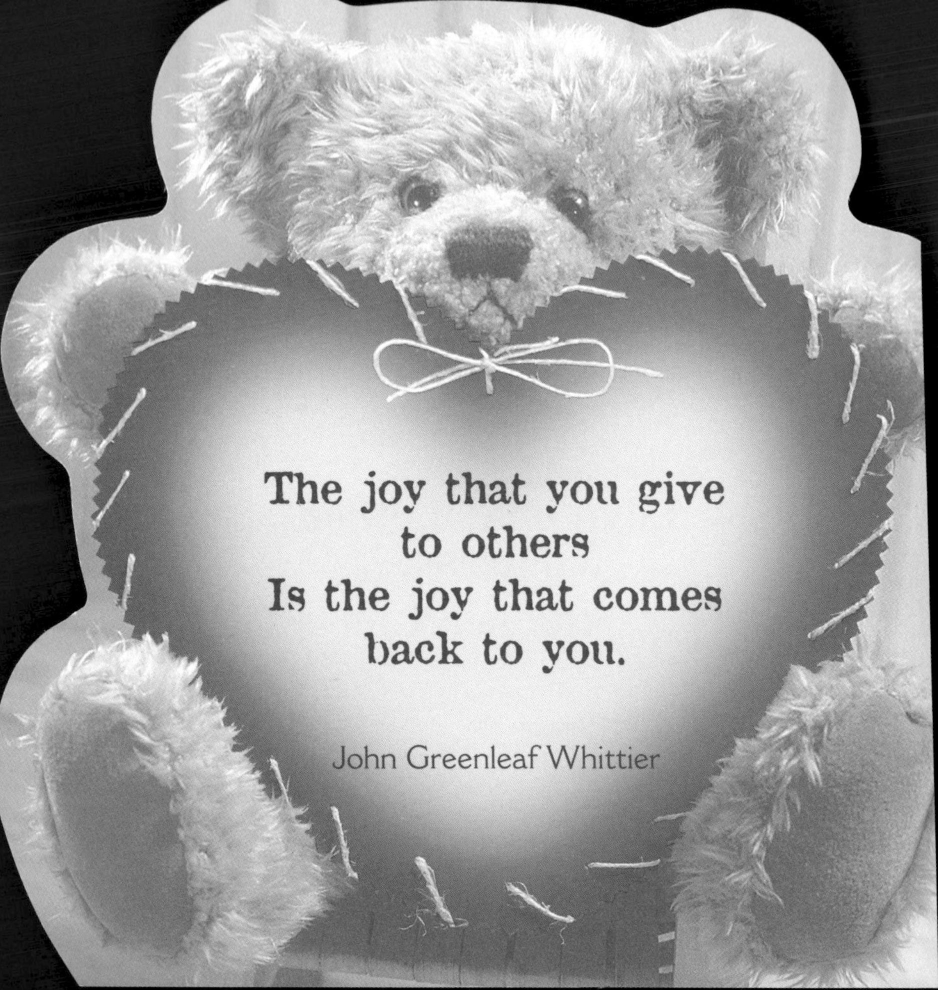

The joy that you give
to others
Is the joy that comes
back to you.

John Greenleaf Whittier

Whoever sows
sparingly will also
reap sparingly, and
whoever sows
generously will also
reap generously.

2 Corinthians 9:6

One who
sows courtesy,
reaps friendship;
One who
plants kindness,
gathers love.

St. Basil

The one who sows to
please the Spirit,
from the Spirit will
reap eternal life.

Galatians 6:8

Our Lord does not care so much for the importance of our works as for the love with which they are done.

Teresa of Avila

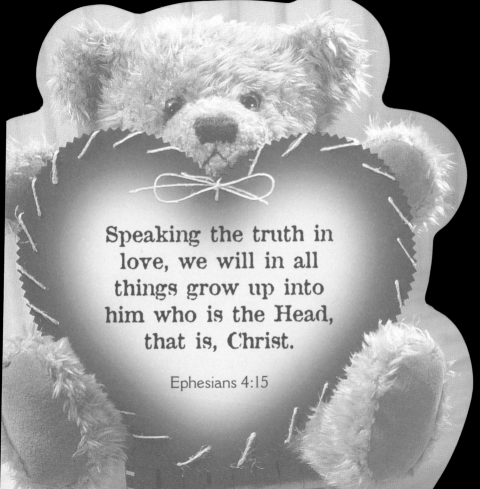

Speaking the truth in love, we will in all things grow up into him who is the Head, that is, Christ.

Ephesians 4:15

Every sincere word of forgiveness we ever speak is a word of God; every generous deed is a service to God's kingdom; and every expression of thanks is a recognition of God's love bestowed through another.

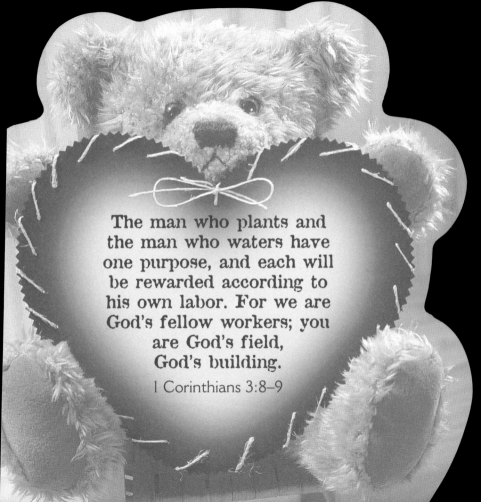

The man who plants and
the man who waters have
one purpose, and each will
be rewarded according to
his own labor. For we are
God's fellow workers; you
are God's field,
God's building.

1 Corinthians 3:8–9

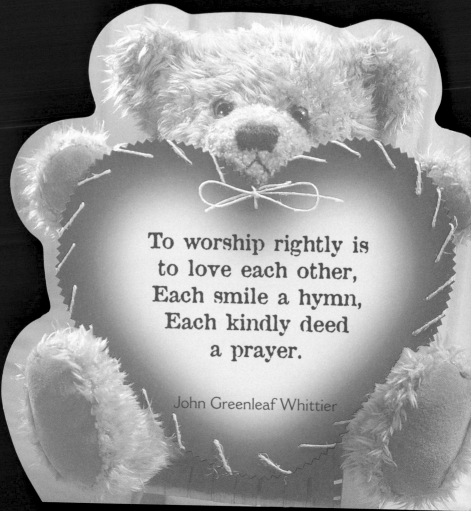

To worship rightly is
to love each other,
Each smile a hymn,
Each kindly deed
a prayer.

John Greenleaf Whittier

Speak to one another with psalms, hymns and spiritual songs. Sing and make music in your heart to the Lord, always giving thanks to God the Father for everything, in the name of our Lord Jesus Christ.

Ephesians 5:19–20

May your right hand
always be stretched
out in friendship, but
never in want.

Irish Proverb

The LORD bless you
and keep you;
the LORD make his face
shine upon you
and be gracious to you;
the LORD turn his face
toward you
and give you peace.

Numbers 6:24–26

For all the blessings
of the year,
For all the friends we
hold so dear,
For peace on earth,
both far and near,
We thank thee, Lord.

Albert H. Hutchinson